Born Again...
To Live

BY

Natasha N. Bell

ISBN:1-59352-166-9

Published by:
Christian Services Network
833 Broadway, Suite #201
El Cajon, CA 92021
Toll Free: 1-866-484-6184
www.CSNbooks.com

Contact Author at:

Natasha N. Bell
2800 NW 56 Avenue, #B-202,
Lauderhill, FL 33313
(954) 530-4077
Email: bornagainbell@yahoo.com

Unless otherwise indicated, all Scripture quotations are taken from the King James Version of the Bible.

Printed in the United States of America.

DEDICATION

I dedicate this book to my daughter Raimi Ceanna Bell whose names mean "God is gracious." Raimi is God's miraculous gift to my husband and I. She is now only 3 years old but I pray that my life will truly resemble the words penned in this book so much that even at a young age she will come to know and have a powerful and intimate relationship with my God, through His Son Jesus Christ, the same Christ Who has saved me from sin, self and the world and continuously delivers me from evil and keeps me and provides for me. I love you, Raimi!!!

ACKNOWLEDGEMENTS

Special thanks, first and foremost, to my Creator God Almighty, Who has such great love toward me, and to His Son, Jesus Christ, Who died a cruel death on a cross that He did not deserve, so that my sins would be forgiven, thus affording me access to abundant and eternal life.

Special thanks to my husband for being patient with me while God was and is teaching, scourging, pruning, and making me all these years of our marriage and more years to come. It is truly an honor to be your wife! Thank you for loving me, encouraging me and helping me.

Special thanks to my mom and dad, Gloria and Lawrence Telfer, for continuously loving me unconditionally in spite of my insolence and ungratefulness during my pre-born-again (teenage and early adult) years.

Special thanks to my pastors (ma & dad) Dr. Ronald C. & Bertha L. Bell, on whose shoulders I have cried many times literally when my soul was burdened deep within with disappointment and sin. Thanks for being my shepherds and "sho-nuff" examples of believers before me. I cannot overemphasize how much of a witness you both are to me! I am eternally grateful to God for you! Thanks for nourishing my soul with the truth of the Word of God. Thank you, thank you, thank you!

TABLE OF CONTENTS

FOREWORD

Why Born Again to Live?

One of the most defining moments in my life was an enlightening experience of sin revealed. Many of us are walking in unrighteousness and refuse to see it and acknowledge it. We do not reverence the men and women of God. We are dishonest and deceive each other so easily because we have turned a deaf ear to the Word when it is preached for so long. We choose not to do what "saith the Lord" as it comes from the oracles of God. We are disobedient and are lovers of pleasure more than lovers of God. I have heard comments such as, "It is just too hard to live a sanctified or holy life," or "I don't want to hear the Word because I will have to be accountable for it." Listen friend, God is not a joke; His Word is true. Yes He is merciful, but He is also faithful and that means you can count on Him to carry out what He said He would do. So when you refuse to hear the Word in whatever way or form that you do so; playing games of ignorance or just doing things your way, which doesn't line up with what the Word of God says or what you are being taught or have been taught by the prophet of the Lord, the Word of the Lord has a message for you:

And because they thought it was worthless to acknowledge God, God allowed their own immoral minds to control them. So they do these indecent things. Their lives are filled with all kinds of sexual sins, wickedness, and greed. They are mean. They are filled with envy, murder, quarreling, deceit, and viciousness. They are gossips, slanderers, haters of God, haughty, arrogant, and boastful. They think up new ways to be cruel. They don't obey their parents, don't have any sense, don't keep promises, and don't show love to their own families or mercy to others. Although they know God's judgment that those who do such things deserve to die, they not only do these things but also approve of others who do them.

(Romans 1:28-32, GW)

The God that we serve today is the same God of Abraham, Isaac and Jacob. He is the same God who sent plagues among the Egyptians and ultimately destroyed Pharoah and his army because they would not let His people go free (read the book of Exodus). He is the same God Who caused Ananias and Sapphira to fall dead because they lied to the Holy Spirit:

But a certain man named Ananias, with Sapphira his wife, sold a possession, and kept back part of the price, his wife also being privy to it, and brought a certain part, and laid it at the apostles' feet. But Peter said, Ananias, why hath Satan filled thine heart to lie to the Holy Ghost, and to keep back part of the price of the land?...thou hast not lied unto men, but unto God. And Ananias hearing these words fell down, and gave up the ghost: and great fear came on all them that heard these things.... And it was about the space of three hours after, when his wife, not knowing what was done, came in. And Peter answered unto her, Tell me whether ye sold the land for so much? And she said, Yea, for so much. Then Peter said unto her, How is it that ye have agreed together to tempt the Spirit of the Lord? behold, the feet of them which have buried thy husband are at the door, and shall carry thee out. Then fell she down straightway at his feet, and yielded up the ghost: and the young men came in, and found her dead, and, carrying her forth, buried her by her husband. And great fear came upon all the church, and upon as many as heard these things.

(Acts 5:1-11)

We are walking in the works of the flesh and loving it. I don't know about you, but that is scary to me. The same God Who gives out blessings also executes judgment in the earth:

And Enoch also, the seventh from Adam, prophesied of these, saying, Behold, the Lord cometh with ten thousands of his saints, to exe-cute judgment upon all, and to convince all that are ungodly among them of all their ungodly deeds which they have ungodly com-mitted, and of all their hard speeches which ungodly sinners have spoken against him.

(Jude 1:14-15)

If we do discern our ungodliness, we turn a blind eye to it because we don't want to be held accountable for it. My friends, it is time to wake up and quit our church-going games (walking in the flesh). It is time to get real with the Almighty God because, according to Galatians 5:21, if we walk in the flesh we will not inherit the Kingdom of God. It is time for us to walk in the fruit of the Spirit, which is love, joy, peace, patience, kindness, goodness, faithfulness, and self-control; and we must exercise this fruit of the Spirit with all people – enemies and friends alike. Someone might be saying, Oh no, I can't get along with my ex-husband/wife, my baby's daddy/momma, my in-laws, that sister/brother in my church, my neighbor, etc. The answer to that is in the words of Jesus in Matthew 5:43-45a:

> *You have heard that it was said, "You shall love your neighbor and hate your enemy." But I say to you, "Love your enemies, bless those who curse you, do good to those who hate you, and pray for those who despitefully use you and persecute you, In this way you show that you are children of your Father in heaven."*

If we do it the other way; hate and have anger and animosity toward those who have hurt us, and especially if they are of the household of faith, then we are showing that we are children of the devil.

1 John 3:10, GW:

> *This is the way God's children are distinguished from the devil's children. Everyone who doesn't do what is right or love other believers isn't God's child.*

It is my prayer that through my testimony and the words penned in this book that every saved and unsaved person throughout every land and country will be changed, delivered, set free, and born again as I have been and then we will all come to the unity of the faith:

> *This is to continue until all of us are united in our faith and in our knowledge about God's Son, until we become mature, until we measure up to Christ, who is the standard.*
>
> (Ephesians 4:13, GW)

CHAPTER ONE

My Testimony

My pastor is also my father-in-law. In my carnal mind I dared to think that he might be biased in his counsel toward me, so in going to him to receive counsel I told him these words: "I don't want you to counsel me as a daughter, daughter-in-law, or as someone you know, I want you to counsel me like a stranger." To sum it up, I was not counseled in the manner that I had expected by my pastor that night but when he left the room I felt like digging a hole right where I was sitting and burying myself. In a matter of seconds, I envisioned myself leaving the church with my daughter and going back to Jamaica where I was born. I told myself, "Yep, this confirms it, they never liked this little ole Jamaican girl from the start." For three days I sought the counsel of God concerning the way that I was feeling toward my pastor and the matter for which I inquired counsel from him. I was delivered by the third day. However, it was not until later on that the Lord revealed to me the prayer of Jonah inside the belly of the whale. I was just awed when I began to read the Scripture through the illumination of the Holy Spirit. The very words of the passage precisely expressed what I had experienced – it was almost unbelievable.

> *Then Jonah prayed unto the LORD his God out of the fish's belly, And said I cried by reason of mine affliction unto the LORD, and he heard me; out of the belly of hell cried I, and thou heardest my voice For thou hadst cast me into the deep, in the midst of the seas; and the floods compassed me about: all thy billows and thy waves passed over me. Then I said, I am cast out of thy sight; yet I will look again toward thy holy temple. The waters compassed me about even to the soul: the depth closed me round about, the weeds were wrapped about my head. I went down to the bottoms of the mountains; the earth with her bars was about me forever: yet hast thou brought up my life from corruption, O LORD my God. When my soul fainted within me I remembered the LORD: and my prayer came in unto thee, into thine holy temple. They that observe lying vanities forsake their own mercy. But I will sacrifice unto thee with the voice of thanksgiving; I will pay that that I have vowed. Salvation is of the LORD. And the LORD spake unto the fish, and it vomited out Jonah upon the dry land.*
> (Jonah 2:1-10)

In our Women's Circle Ministry at my church we studied a topic that I had to speak on entitled "Conflict – Opportunity for Growth" and believe me it is. The word conflict means: a "state of opposition between persons, or ideas or interests." Some common synonyms are: struggle, disunity, war or friction. I have found that my most flourishing spiritual growth took place in the midst of or after conflict. Although it is an opportunity for growth it is also an opportunity for decline, but I was and am determined that my choice will be growth and not decline because the Lord has no pleasure in a draw-back spirit. Each time there is conflict going on in my life I am reminded that my warfare is not against flesh and blood, but against the devil himself and so I fight not with the tools of the flesh but with the weapons of the Spirit which God Himself has authorized:

> *This is not a wrestling match against a human opponent. We are wrestling with rulers, authorities, the powers who govern this world of darkness, and spiritual forces that control evil in the heavenly world. For this reason, take up all the armor that God supplies. Then you will be able to take a stand during these evil days. Once you have overcome all obstacles, you will be able to stand your ground. So then, take your stand! Fasten truth around your waist like a belt. Put on God's approval as your breastplate. Put on your shoes so that you are ready to spread the Good News that gives peace. In addition to all these, take the Christian faith as your shield. With it you can put out all the flaming arrows of the evil one. Also take salvation as your helmet and the word of God as the sword that the Spirit supplies. Pray in the Spirit in every situation. Use every kind of prayer and request there is.*
>
> (Ephesians 6:12-18, GW)

Some time after this situation I was having a conversation with someone and the tone of the conversation with this person was revealed to be one of irreverence for the man of God. This was such an eye opener for me. I immediately began to look at myself and really became so awed and frightened by the experience. The Lord began to show me my own disregard and disrespect of my pastor in a way that I had not seen it before. On Sunday August 1, 2004 I was awakened at 2:30 am by the voice of the Lord, which instructed me to begin writing.

So I began by researching Ephesians 4:11-32: And truly He gave some to be apostles...prophets...evangelists...pastors and teachers. I also began researching the meaning of the word pastor. He then instructed me to write what is now written in these pages - my testimony. I felt a relentless unction to share this confession and testimony with the church but I wanted to be in order so I waited for a chance to ask my pastor's permission to speak. Well, I did not get the opportunity to ask his permission privately, so I petitioned God for some form of confirmation that it would have been okay to speak during or after the service. God gave the confirmation and so I decided to do it during the evening service when we would be partaking of the Holy Communion. God again gave confirmation. Once the service was coming to a close, opportunity was granted. I must tell you that I was faced with several attacks from the enemy throughout the day because he saw the benefit of what I was about to do and he wanted to put a stop to it, but I was determined to be obedient and make an open confession of my sin. I was in awe with the events that followed my confession but it only confirms that the Lord is faithful to His Word, in that He says,

If my people, which are called by my name, shall humble themselves, and pray, and seek my face, and turn from their wicked ways; then will I hear from heaven, and will forgive their sin, and will heal their land.

(2 Chronicles 7:14)

After I went to sleep that night and awoke Monday morning, the Holy Spirit spoke to me in that still small voice of His and said, "Born Again." I couldn't understand it but I actually felt like a brand new person and have been feeling that way ever since. Someone may feel that I have not been on this road for a long time, and what could I possibly know, but I have come to find out one thing in life, and it is that quality is far better than quantity. So it does not matter how many years you have been saved but the quality of your salvation. Are you walking in a newness of life continuously? Are you walking in obedience to the Lord? Of course that does not mean that there will no longer be troubles or trials that come upon you like a whirlwind and seem to almost knock you to the ground and cause you to feel as though you will never survive. But when these troubles come, and they will once you have been born again, you are assured of who you are in Christ, the one who sacrificed His life so that you can indeed LIVE. Regardless of how you may feel you can say with confidence the words of the Psalmist.

I shall not die, but live, and declare the works of the LORD. The LORD hath chastened me sore: but he hath not given me over unto death.

(Psalm 118:17-18)

19

Whoever you are reading this book, I want to sincerely express to you that it is a dangerous thing to think that you know more than your pastor. How can you possibly know more than someone whom God has designated to watch over your soul? Unless you don't really believe that God is in control or that the person who is your pastor is not really anointed by God to do the task. If the latter is the case I suggest you seek God in a mighty way to guide you to someone who is anointed to pastor you. Contrary to popular belief the office of the pastor has not been played out – it is the pastor's duty to give an account and to care for your soul according to God's will and purpose until the Lord says differently. The guidance of a pastor is very important in the nurturing of your soul. Often times through the inspiration of the Holy Spirit the pastor is able to see danger farther down on the path that you may have decided to travel. It is his duty to warn you and govern you to safety with all of the ability that God has bestowed upon him or her. We often resent the warnings and the scourgings but it behooves us to take heed of the oracles of God. I know that we can have some really great opinions and feelings at times, but they really don't matter when it comes to the Word of the Lord. Unfortunately, feelings and opinions are the main boogers that cause us to mis-step in so many ways.

As the Lord began to reveal these things to me He further began to show me the connection between the way we relate to our earthly fathers and to our spiritual fathers. That made me realize even more how important it is to have a respectful relationship with one's father in regard to our relationship with the Lord (refer to Hebrews 12). The Lord showed me that I could not even possibly know how to reverence my spiritual Father because I had not known how to reverence my earthly father. You see, I was very unruly as a child. My parents told me that things were to be a certain way but "I thought" it ought to go differently. Here I am, a child knowing better than my parents. I always had an opinion or feeling about how things should or should not go and honey let me tell you, I voiced it too. I would speak and throw my words – I didn't call any names but I spoke with a tone of voice and content, which made even the deaf know that I was talking about you. The relationship with one's father is so important in so many ways. It depicts how we relate to our husbands, our pastors, our Lord, and others in authority. I'll take a moment to say that if you have not had a healthy relationship with your father now is the time for healing. This is just so awesome the way that God has ordained His creation. Everything has an order. Children are to obey and honor their parents. The same thing that He tells the saints (who are referred to as children, by the way) is to obey the Pastors and to give them not just regular honor but double honor. Many of us are unable to do this very basic of tasks because we think we are "grown." That is the first thing a person will say when it comes down to someone telling them to do something, especially if it is something that they do not want to do. But we can't be grown in the house of the Lord because He has commanded us through His Scriptures to become as little children:

> *Truly I say to you, unless you are converted and become as little children, you shall not enter into the kingdom of Heaven.*
> (Matthew 18:3, MKJV)

21

The Scripture says that we must be converted. What in the world does that mean? Converted means to change something into another form, substance, state, or product, transform; the antonym is unchanged. So if you are not a changed believer, if there is no change in your whole being from that of the sinful state that you were born in, according to the Scriptures you shall not enter into the Kingdom of Heaven.

Why is it that we hate changing so much when Jesus Himself tells us we need to? Many people who have accepted Christ as their Savior and vow to serve Him all the days of their lives don't like preachers who stress that there must be a change. It is said that those who remain under such leadership are under bondage. When we were in the world and of the world we were free to indulge in whatever brought pleasure to us. We were big and bad enough to do it our way. Saints, I exhort you that it is not so once you've accepted Christ as your Savior. Paul refers to us and to the saints of his time as soldiers:

> *I feel that I must send Epaphroditus – my brother, coworker, and fellow soldier-back to you. You sent him as your personal representative to help me in my need.*
> (Philippians 2:25, GW)

> *Join me in suffering like a good soldier of Christ Jesus. Whoever serves in the military doesn't get mixed up in non-military activities. This pleases his commanding officer.*
> (2 Timothy 2:3-4, GW)

> *...our sister Apphia, our fellow soldier Archippus, and the church that meets in your house.*
> (Philemon 1:2, GW)

If you know the criteria of a soldier in a natural army you'll know that a soldier must be trained, must wear his uniform and must be prepared to go out to battle when called upon. You must be released from the army in which you have enlisted by a higher order; if you do otherwise you will be branded for life as a dishonorably discharged soldier if you violated the rules and code of conduct or one that went AWOL – meaning you ran away. Saints, it works very much the same in the Christian world.

Saints, there must be a change! Just like the caterpillar changes into a beautiful butterfly, so it is that we must be changed into a new creation. Old things must be passed away and behold all things must become new. I remember doing some soul searching about the way I had behaved with one of my neighbors. I thought to myself, how could I be a witness of Christ to a person who is a sinner when I am handling a situation just as they are? It couldn't be, not if I were to be a witness. I had to be different, not just because I go to church and they don't, or because they wear pants and I don't. There must be an inward change, and the inward change will reflect on the outside. Your desires will change, even the way you dress will change. You are no longer dressing with the intent to have someone lust after you, to see how fine you are or how sexy you look. You even begin to dress shame-faced, as the Scripture tells us,

> *And I want women to get in there with the men in humility before God, not primping before a mirror or chasing the latest fashions, but doing something beautiful for God and becoming beautiful doing it.*

> (1 Timothy 2:9-10, MSG)

I told a dear friend of mine some time ago that I am constantly learning to do things differently. Later on the Holy Spirit helped me to understand that the mind had to be in constant renewal. You see, there are ways that seem right to a man but the end leads to death, and I dare say a spiritual death.

There is a way that seems right to a man, but its end is the way of death.
(Proverbs 14:12, NKJV)

We have some ways in which we do things, or how we think something ought to go at times, but they will eventually lead to death; they will be unproductive in our lives and I have had to renew my thinking in many areas of my life, even though it seemed right to me at the time. Friends, the Scripture tells us that we ought to renew our minds from the way that we used to think about things and do things:

Because you are children who obey God, don't live the kind of lives you once lived. Once you lived to satisfy your desires because you didn't know any better.
(1 Peter 1:14, GW)

You were taught to change the way you were living. The person you used to be will ruin you through desires that deceive you.
(Ephesians 4:22, GW)

God has orchestrated all of our lives and until we begin to see things as God sees them we will never realize our destiny, we will never experience LIFE and that more abundantly – the plan that God has ordained for our lives.

The thief does not come except to steal, and to kill, and to destroy. I have come that they may have life, and that they may have it more abundantly.

(John 10:10, NKJV)

The first thing to realize is that God loves the world so much that He has given His only Son to die a cruel and shameful death in order for whoever believes on Him to experience the free gift of salvation – "Eternal & Abundant Life."

I have no idea why I am even writing this. However, all of this has been able to come forth because of the teaching of my pastors and the love and support of my husband Rawlinds. I am a by-product of the ministry of Dr. Ronald C. and Bertha L. Bell.

On Wednesday, September 29, 2004 I received a prophetic word from Bishop Dr. William Lee, pastor of Pillar of Fire Refuge Church. He told me that he saw me writing a book, a best seller, selling one million copies. That was quite a holy-incidence since earlier that day, before hearing the word of the prophet, I said these words to my husband, "Hon, I feel as though I am writing a book, I don't understand it and I can't explain it but I just feel as though I am writing a book."

The writing of this book has been prophetically ordained by God; so it is my prayer that whoever you are reading this book that has been truly penned by the inspiration of the Holy Spirit, that you come to experience what I have by the grace of God, and that is to be **born again**.

What shall we say then...can you say with assurance that you are born again? If not, what are you willing to do about it?

_____

_____

_____

Are you experiencing the joy of the Lord, or has your salvation become dull, lifeless and boring to you? What are you willing to do to make a change?

_____

_____

_____

CHAPTER TWO

What Does it Mean to Be Born Again?

What does it mean to be born again? Well, Nicodemus asked the question,

How can a man be born when he is old? Can he enter the second time into his mother's womb and be born? Jesus answered,

Truly, truly, I say to you, unless a man is born of water and the Spirit, he cannot enter into the kingdom of God. That which is born of the flesh is flesh, and that which is born of the Spirit is spirit. Do not marvel that I said to you, you must be born again. The Spirit breathes where He desires, and you hear His voice, but you do not know from where He comes, and where He goes; so is everyone who is born of the Spirit.

(John 3:4-8, MKJV)

Yes we are born of the flesh from our mother's womb, but in Christ we must be reborn of the Spirit. We must go through a newness of life. When a mother gives birth she gives birth to a brand new baby. This baby must learn how to eat, walk, run and be guided to a full stature of maturity. It is the same with a spiritual birth. You are now a new creature, as Paul stated,

> *Now we look inside, and what we see is that anyone united with the Messiah gets a fresh start, is created new. The old life is gone; a new life burgeons! Look at it!*
> (2 Corinthians 5:17, MSG)

That means old habits or the way you used to do things, attitudes, conduct, etc., plainly put, works of the flesh, are no longer a part of your character. Your character must resemble your Savior and Father. But why is it that many believers or those who are claiming to have received the gift of salvation still have the same old behaviors as they did before they were born again? If you are the same person that you were before you were born again I challenge you that if you are not a member of a church where change is necessary, that you ask to be released so that you can plant yourself in such a church where you can be nurtured just as a babe is and you can be guided toward the full stature of your spiritual maturity. There are many churches out there where the pastor has the credentials to guide you in this manner. If you truly want a transformed life begin to seek God's guidance – ask Him to direct you to a church that is going to nurture your spirit man.

In the process of a spiritual re-birth it is very important to have good parents, just as in the natural.

I am truly grateful for my pastors who are my spiritual parents. And as parents they teach, pastor, nurture, feed and oversee.

> *And truly He gave some to be apostles, and some to be prophets, and some to be evangelists and some to be pastors and teachers, for the perfecting of the saints, for the work of the ministry, for the edifying of the body of Christ. And this until we all come into the unity of the faith and of the knowledge of the Son of God, to a full-grown man, to the measure of the stature of the fullness of Christ; so that we no longer may be infants, tossed to and fro and carried about by every wind of doctrine, in the dishonesty of men, in cunning craftiness, to the wiles of deceit.*
>
> (Ephesians 4:11-14, MKJV)

The definition of pastor is "one who defends the flock against the enemy, causes the flock to rest, accounts for the flock, knows each one of his flock by name, keeps the sheep and goats apart, waters the flock, keeps the flocks in fold, watches over the flock, a spiritual overseer, minister of the Holy Spirit and Word and nourishes and cherishes the flock."

In turn, the sheep or children (the Scripture says unless we come as little children we can in no wise enter in) under his care should respond in obedience according to Hebrews,

> *...obey those who rule over you and be submissive, for they watch out for your souls, as those who must give account.*
>
> (Hebrews 13:17, NKJV)

In watching out for our souls it may sometimes involve exhorting against sin. Exhorting usually involves correction. Correction isn't easy to take but it is necessary for our spiritual growth. Those who accept it and are improved by it will receive a good reward, this is so stated in Hebrews 12:9-11, MKJV:

Furthermore we have had fathers of our flesh who corrected us and we gave them reverence. Shall we not much rather be in subjection to the Father of Spirits and live? For truly they chastened us for a few days according to their own pleasure but He for our profit, that we might be partakers of His holiness. Now chastening for the present does not seem to be joyous, but grievous. Nevertheless afterward it yields the peaceable fruit of righteousness to those who are exercised by it.

One evening my husband and I and our pastors (who are also my husband's parents) and my husband's brother and his wife went to see "The Passion of the Christ" and then sat down at a restaurant to eat dinner. While waiting for our meal my husband began to kid around, as he always does, and in my mind I was thinking how could he behave in such a way. We just finished watching a replica of what our Savior went through for us. And I began to feel disgust at his behavior because I thought he should be solemn and reflecting upon what Christ had to go through. I was so busy judging his behavior that I could not see the stench of mine. Suddenly my pastor said to me, "You know if you were rich you would be 'stank.'" For those who don't know, "stank" is like the worst part on the totem pole of being "stink." Days and weeks went by and the statement my pastor made kept ringing in my spirit – I was very unsettled by it. The statement was continuously playing back in my mind and then I began to seek the Lord concerning what he said and the Lord showed me that it was indeed true. What was going on inside of me was made manifest on the outside. I repented bitterly because that was not a characteristic of Jesus, whom I wanted to be like.

In my born again experience I have come to realize the vast importance of the pastor and giving reverence to a pastor. There are many who don't really like the words that my pastor preaches, but that makes me wonder because the words that my pastor preaches are from the Scriptures. Some seem to think that he is too harsh, but guess what – so was Jesus in the way that He spoke to many who crossed His path while He traveled and in the words that He has left for us to follow. Yes Jesus was full of compassion but remember when He began calling people to be His disciples? One man said that he had to go bury his father and Jesus' response was "Let the dead bury the dead" – how harsh was that! Another said that he was just married and needed to go let his wife know that he was leaving and His response was "no man that taketh hold to the plow and looketh back is fit for the kingdom" – how harsh was that!

And He said to another, Follow Me! But he said, Lord, first allow me to go and bury my father. Jesus said to him, Let the dead bury their dead, but you go and proclaim the kingdom of God. And another also said, Lord, I will follow You, but first allow me to take leave of those in my house. And Jesus said to him, No one, having put his hand to the plow and looking back, is fit for the kingdom of God.
(Luke 9:59-62, MKJV)

31

Yet another time he said,

Anyone who comes to me but refuses to let go of father, mother, spouse, children, brothers, sisters – yes, even one's own self! – can't be my disciple. Anyone who won't shoulder his own cross and follow behind me can't be my disciple.

(Luke 14:26-27 MSG)

How harsh is that? What is meant here, is that whenever loving spouse, children, father, mother and even self come in conflict with honoring Christ and His Word, and you choose self or family or friend over Christ, then you can't be His disciple because a disciple's desire would be to choose Christ. Mother, father, etc. may be hurt and it may hurt you also, but there is an eternal reward for choosing Christ as is stated in Mark 10:29-30:

And Jesus answered and said, Verily I say unto you, There is no man that hath left house, or brethren, or sisters, or father, or mother, or wife, or children, or lands, for my sake, and the gospel's, But he shall receive a hundredfold now in this time, houses, and brethren, and sisters, and mothers, and children, and lands, with persecutions; and in the world to come eternal life.

When Jesus calls us into this born again life, He is calling us into a life of change and repentance not only for ourselves but also unto those with whom we come in contact. Because of our changed lives, others will be changed. We are not born again simply so that we can have a personal relationship with Jesus Christ and His Father, but also so that we can live as witnesses of Christ in the earth. Through our witness lives can be changed. Friends, this will only happen through our complete and unhesitant obedience to the Word of Christ, which is God's order. Our response every day should be just like that of Simon-Peter and Andrew and James and John shown here in Matthew 4:18-22:

> *Walking along the beach of Lake Galilee, Jesus saw two brothers: Simon (later called Peter) and Andrew. They were fishing, throwing their nets into the lake. It was their regular work. Jesus said to them, "Come with me. I'll make a new kind of fisherman out of you. I'll show you how to catch men and women instead of perch and bass." They didn't ask questions, but simply dropped their nets and followed. A short distance down the beach they came upon another pair of brothers, James and John, Zebedee's sons. These two were sitting in a boat with their father, Zebedee, mending their fishnets. Jesus made the same offer to them, and they were just as quick to follow, abandoning boat and father.*

(Matthew 4:18-22)

What about you? Are you born again? If yes, are you just as quick to follow Jesus, abandoning family, friends, opinions, ideas and self? Be completely honest while searching yourself and write your response below. Remember, in order to be healed we must first know and confess that there is a problem. We must first empty ourselves in order to be filled. What steps will you commit to make in order to truly experience being born again?

CHAPTER THREE

No More Self-Righteousness

A born again believer has no business being self-righteous, yet it seems to be the most prevalent of attitudes among those who claim to be born again believers, sanctified, and filled with the Holy Ghost. We tend to look down on others who are claiming the same faith if they don't look the same as we do. The Holy Spirit revealed this to me about myself. The Lord brought the Scripture to my mind and spoke directly to me. He said you are a whitewashed sepulcher full of dead men's bones. Why? Because I was all caught up in the fact that I wore a hat for my covering and my skirts and dresses were long enough so that I was not showing too much "meat," and I did not wear earrings or any extra jewelry, etc.

But in the same manner that I judged because I thought I was so righteous, those that do not see themselves conforming to the old holiness way of life, judge those who do. All around, friends, God is not pleased. He is the only one who judges, but be careful that you become too lapse and begin to think in your mind, oh yeah, no one can judge me. Be very careful that you are standing on the Word of God because the Scripture does tell us how to adorn ourselves, speak and behave ourselves. So whether someone is judging us unjustly or not we must make sure that we are standing on holy ground in the Word of God. Take a deep look at the following Scripture:

Submit yourselves therefore to God. Resist the devil, and he will flee from you. Draw nigh to God, and he will draw nigh to you. Cleanse your hands, ye sinners; and purify your hearts, ye double minded...Speak not evil one of another, brethren. He that speaketh evil of his brother, and judgeth his brother, speaketh evil of the law, and judgeth the law: but if thou judge the law, thou art not a doer of the law, but a judge. There is one lawgiver, who is able to save and to destroy: who art thou that judgest another?

(James 4:7-12)

The Pharisee syndrome, as I have called it, is nothing more than thinking of yourself more highly than you ought to. I know that syndrome very well, and the Lord through His grace and mercy revealed it to me in a most profound way. I had been very judgmental toward someone for a very long time. I saw this person through the eyes of the flesh and not of the spirit. There were so many things about this person that disturbed me: the way she walked, talked, her facial expressions, you name it. To avoid it I began to try not to look her in the face so that I would not see her expressions. I tried to counteract my feelings by reaching out to this person but this booger just would not go away. I now became desperate to get rid of this feeling that I was having, I wanted to be able to feel free when dealing with this person, so I decided to embark on a week of fasting from 6:00 am to 6:00 pm – no food or drink. A very dear friend of mine, and a partner in faith, joined me on the fast – we were going to touch and agree in order for the Lord to sho' nuff hear us. The Monday when we began the fast I read Isaiah 58 (I like to read Scriptures regarding fasting when I am fasting) and put the Bible down and went throughout the day. I spoke to my prayer partner at the end of the fast, we blessed each other and were looking forward to the following day. I had not told my prayer partner that I had read that Scripture the previous day, but she called me Tuesday mid morning and told me to read the very same Scripture that I had read the previous day. When I read the Scripture the Lord spoke to me so clearly through verse 6:

> *This is the kind of fasting I have chosen: Loosen the chains of wickedness, untie the straps of the yoke, let the oppressed go free, and break every yoke. (GW).*

Immediately I began to weep before the Lord because I was guilty of holding a yoke around this person's neck for them to do right but the Lord wanted me to break every yoke. Isaiah 58:9: *Then you will call, and the LORD will answer. You will cry for help, and he will say, "Here I am!"* Get rid of that yoke. Don't point your finger and say wicked things.

Matthew 5:20 began to be very real to me:

> *For I say unto you, that except your righteousness shall exceed the righteousness of the*

scribes and Pharisees, ye shall in no case enter into the kingdom of heaven.

Then came Matthew 23:13,

But woe unto you, scribes and Pharisees, hypocrites! For ye shut up the kingdom of heaven against men: for ye neither go in yourselves, neither suffer ye them that are entering to go in.

This made me realize that being a hypocrite or being self-righteous would not only cause me not to enter the Kingdom of Heaven but that I would "shut up the kingdom of heaven against men."

Matthew 23:27,

How horrible it will be for you, scribes and Pharisees! You hypocrites! You are like whitewashed graves that look beautiful on the outside but inside are full of dead people's bones and every kind of impurity (GW).

Matthew 23:23

How horrible it will be for you, scribes and Pharisees! You hypocrites! You give God one-tenth of your mint, dill, and cumin. But you have neglected justice, mercy, and faithfulness. These are the most important things in Moses' Teachings. You should have done these things without neglecting the others (GW).

While self-righteousness may be displayed through an arrogant and proud attitude, it is not the substance of it. It is possible, and I submit quite prevalent, that a person who is self-righteous can appear to be humble.

Self-righteousness is not just an attitude but a way of living. It is to live life with the goal of self-improvement. For a Christian, this would mean that their goal is to improve themselves in order to be more pleasing to God. Christians have used the word "sanctification" to describe their pursuit of pleasing God.

At the heart of all these pursuits is the goal to become more righteous, more acceptable, and more pleasing. These pursuits are also characterized by the efforts of the person. Thus we have the pursuit of self to be more righteous – get it-self-righteousness.

The typical Evangelical understanding about how to live life is to figure out what is right and wrong and then to do what is right. Wasn't this the essence of the very first temptation presented by Satan? Satan told Eve that she could know the difference between right and wrong. This ability to know implies that they could choose to do what is right. They were deceived into thinking they could be "right" on their own. They could be like God and be right! I believe that we are actually promoting the very sin that brought about the fall of man. Self-righteousness is to determine for us what is right and then to do it.

It is a good thing to want to be pleasing to others and to God. Within all of us is a craving within our hearts to be acceptable. We desperately seek a rock solid relationship of acceptance among our peers. The desire to please God is also a fruit of God's life in a person, but let us not confuse the desire to please God with a life that is lived trying to please Him.

We cannot become acceptable in our own right. This is partly what makes self-righteousness so atrocious. We have created for ourselves a goal which can never be met. This pursuit of self-righteousness is what empowers Satan to be the "accuser of the brethren." And so it is that those of us who are adamant about how righteous we are and tend to accuse those who don't seem to measure up according to our standards.

The teaching and pursuit of self-righteousness in the church is the explanation for most of the apathy and lack of joy among Christians. We have created a toxic environment where standards are raised and often not followed. Some people leave, knowing they are not measuring up. Some pretend they are living right and are miserable. Many are waiting for the "key" that will finally cause them to live holy. Many have tuned out any sense of true spirituality and have ceased to let any truth penetrate. Some are deceived into thinking they are measuring up! Isaiah declares that our righteousness is as filthy rags.

We must settle this issue of righteousness, as did the Apostle Paul in his letter to the Philippians. He wrote, "That I may be found in Him, not having a righteousness of my own derived from the Law, but that which is through faith in Christ, the righteousness which comes from God on the basis of faith." Let us also remember the words of Jesus in Matthew 5:20: *For I say unto, that except your righteousness shall exceed the righteousness of the scribes and Pharisees, ye shall in no case enter into the kingdom of heaven.*

There is only one way to deal with this basic of all sins. We must rest from the pursuit of self-righteousness. We must accept the gift of His righteousness. It is finished – everyone in Christ (abiding in Him and allowing His Word to abide in you) is holy, blameless and fully acceptable to God. The key point here is living a life obeying His Word and doing what He has required of us, not what we have made up in our minds to do or what someone else has made up for us to do.

> *He hath shewed thee, O man, what is good; and what doth the LORD require of thee, but to do justly, and to love mercy, and to walk humbly with thy God?*
>
> (Micah 6:8)

To do justly means to deal honestly and with benevolence, and to do that which is beneficial to the receiver.

To love mercy means to embrace being compassionate and lenient, to forbear and to deal with gentleness. I must take a little time with the word forbear because it means to bear someone before they even need you to bear them. This is extremely awesome and powerful!

To walk humbly with thy God means that your position or disposition is one of submissive respect and honor for God. Your attitude is one of meekness, not arrogance or pride.

I am convinced that if Christians could actually embrace **Christ's righteousness** alone, we would witness a revolution in the Church. No longer would we be like the Pharisees who were more concerned about the washing of the hands; the outward appearances and acts but we would concern ourselves with the spirit and the content of the heart.

HERE ARE SOME TRUTHS ABOUT SELF-RIGHTEOUSNESS:

● The "self-righteous" are, as the Lord puts it, *"those who trust in themselves that they are righteous, and despise others."* (Luke 18:9).

● Self-righteousness is a sore evil because it is difficult to detect.

● It is especially hard for us to notice when we are guilty of it ourselves.

HERE ARE SOME WAYS TO AVOID AND ERADICATE SELF-RIGHTEOUSNESS IN OUR LIVES:

1. Give God the glory for every accomplishment, and in all things.

We ought not to seek our own glory or the glory of man, but rather seek (earnestly looking for it with all of our heart) His glory. We give Him all the glory, not just with lip service, but from within, from the heart.

He that speaketh of himself seeketh his own glory: but he that seeketh his glory that sent him, the same is true, and no unrighteousness is in him.

(John 7:18)

Another reason why we should give all the glory to God and not ourselves is that we will become consumed by the worms of self-righteousness.

And immediately the angel of the Lord smote him, because he gave not God the glory: and he was eaten of worms, and gave up the ghost.

(Acts 12:23)

2. Be genuinely concerned about the brethren.

We then that are strong ought to bear the infirmities of the weak, and not to please ourselves. Let every one of us please his neighbor for his good to edification. For even Christ pleased not himself.

(Romans 15:1-3a)

3. Love one another.

A new commandment I give unto you, That ye love one another; as I have loved you, that ye also love one another. By this shall all men know that ye are my disciples, if ye have love one to another.

(John 13:34-35)

Beloved, let us love one another: for love is of God; and every one that loveth is born of God, and knoweth God. He that loveth not knoweth not God; for God is love.

(1 John 4:7-8)

If ye fulfil the royal law according to the Scripture, Thou shalt love thy neighbor as thyself, ye do well: But if ye have respect to persons, ye commit sin, and are convinced of the law as transgressors.

(James 2:8-9)

43

When you love someone you are always moved to doing something good for that person. Well the Scripture also directs us in doing good, especially for those whom we call brethren.

As we have therefore opportunity, let us do good unto all men, especially unto them who are of the household of faith.

(Galatians 6:10)

4. Recognize and acknowledge complete and total dependence on Christ.

For when we were yet without strength, in due time Christ died for the ungodly. For scarcely for a righteous man will one die: yet peradventure for a good man some would even dare to die. But God commendeth his love toward us, in that, while we were yet sinners, Christ died for us. Much more then, being now justified by his blood, we shall be saved from wrath through him. For if, when we were enemies, we were reconciled to God by the death of his Son, much more, being reconciled, we shall be saved by his life. And not only so, but we also joy in God through our Lord Jesus Christ, by whom we have now received the atonement.

(Romans 5:6-11)

Were it not for Christ and His death on our behalf, every sin and stain would still be with us; we would still be sinners without strength and without access to eternal life.

5. Consider others better than us.

Don't act out of selfish ambition or be conceited. Instead, humbly think of others as being better than yourselves. Don't be concerned only about your own interests, but also be concerned about the interests of others.

(Philippians 2:3-4, GW)

Love from the center of who you are; don't fake it. Run for dear life from evil; hold on for dear life to good. Be good friends who love deeply; practice playing second fiddle.

(Romans 12:9-10, MSG)

Playing second fiddle is something that many of us don't like to do because we have an in-born nature within us that loves to be seen and loves to be first. Playing second fiddle allows the other person to get credit. This simple instruction from God's Word will help us to keep from looking down our noses at others and also weaken the potency of pride and self-right-eousness, which I believe are second cousins to each other. When we are **genuinely** concerned about the problems and needs of our fellow Christians, we will not be self-righteous.

6. Be doers and not only hearers of God's Word.

Wherefore lay apart all filthiness and super-fluity of naughtiness, and receive with meekness the engrafted word, which is able to save your souls. But be ye doers of the word, and not hearers only, deceiving your own selves. For if any be a hearer of the word, and not a doer, he is like unto a man beholding his natural face in a glass: For he beholdeth himself, and goeth his way, and straightway forgetteth what man-ner of man he was. But whoso looketh into the perfect law of liberty, and continueth therein, he being not a forgetful hearer, but a doer of the work, this man shall be blessed in his deed.

(James 1:21-25)

We must make an honest, diligent effort in applying His Word to our lives. Be taught the Word of God by a pastor – one who is concerned for the saving of your soul. When you get to the house of the Lord, have your heart and mind set and ready to receive the Word with a willingness to practice what is preached, even if it hurts. If something may not be clear to you, seek the counsel of God through profound prayer and your pastors.

Lord who shall abide in thy tabernacle...he that sweareth to his own hurt and changeth not.

(Psalm 15:1-4)

To be a doer of God's Word you must be faithful whatever the cost; and it will cost you.

7. Learn, develop, and practice humility.

Humility speaks of being meek and submissive and modest in one's behavior, not arrogant or prideful. One of the glaring, evident problems with the Pharisees was their arrogance and pride – their self-righteousness. In His parable against the self-righteous, Jesus showed the importance of humility.

And he spake this parable unto certain which trusted in themselves that they were righteous, and despised others: Two men went up into the temple to pray; the one a Pharisee, and the other a publican. The Pharisee stood and prayed thus with himself, God, I thank thee, that I am not as other men are, extortioners, unjust, adulterers, or even as this publican. I fast twice in the week, I give tithes of all that I possess. And the publican, standing afar off, would not lift up so much as his eyes unto heaven, but smote upon his breast, saying, God be merciful to me a sinner. I tell you, this man went down to his house justified rather than the other: for every one that exalteth himself shall be abased; and he that humbleth himself shall be exalted.

(Luke 18:9-14)

If you are determined to be proud and exalt yourself – give the impression that you are better than others in the way you speak, what you say, and how you behave, God Almighty will bring you to a low place – He will humble you and that, my friend, will not be pleasant. God resists (stands firm against) those who are proud, haughty, high-minded and exalted, but He finds pleasure in those who are humble.

Likewise, ye younger, submit yourselves unto the elder. Yea, all of you be subject one to another, and be clothed with humility: for God resisteth the proud, and giveth grace to the humble. Humble yourselves therefore under the mighty hand of God, that he may exalt you in due time.

(1 Peter 5:5-7)

8. Turn the other cheek.

We must be willing to turn the other cheek or vacate ourselves and our "rights," for example, when we are insulted, accused wrongfully, or asked to give up that which rightfully belongs to us. My pastor preached a message entitled "Nice Guys Finish Last...but They Finish." Turning the other cheek is something for the nice guys or the pushovers to do. It doesn't matter in what position we finish, as long as we finish. Many of us are reared with the ideal that "I'm not going to let anyone take advantage of me." As women, we are taught not to let any man get the best of us but this attitude is one of pride and "me first." Let us hear what "saith the Lord" in the matter as He calls us higher unto perfection.

> *Ye have heard that it hath been said, An eye for an eye, and a tooth for a tooth: But I say unto you, That ye resist not evil: but whosoever shall smite thee on thy right cheek, turn to him the other also. And if any man will sue thee at the law, and take away thy coat, let him have thy cloke also. And whosoever shall compel thee to go a mile, go with him twain. Give to him that asketh thee, and from him that would borrow of thee turn not thou away. Ye have heard that it hath been said, Thou shalt love thy neighbor, and hate thine enemy. But I say unto you, Love your enemies, bless them that curse you, do good to them that hate you, and pray for them which despitefully use you, and persecute you; That ye may be the children of your Father which is in heaven:...Be ye therefore perfect, even as your Father which is in heaven is perfect.*

> (Matthew 5:38-48)

As wives many of us have a difficult time submitting to our husbands, as the Scripture tells us to, because of what has been instilled within us for so many years by our parents, friends, and relatives.

48

And husbands as well have the same difficulty. I, myself, had that same mentality. I desperately wanted to be a submissive wife and so on the surface I was, until my God and Father, my deliverer, delivered me. It is a tremendous blessing to be able to walk in the freedom of God's Word, for truly it is the perfect law of liberty. It has come to set us free from these paradigms of life that have us bound from birth until death. I am now able to say with true conviction just like Christ said, "No man takes my life from me, because I lay it down." My husband cannot take anything from me; he cannot take advantage of me, because I lay my life down for him.

> *Therefore doth my Father love me, because I lay down my life, that I might take it again. No man taketh it from me, but I lay it down of myself. I have power to lay it down, and I have power to take it again.*
>
> (John 10:17-18)

It is the most awesome experience!!! Jesus said no greater love is there than a man laying down his life for a friend, and because I am my husband's friend, and a friend to the brethren at home or abroad I lay down my life for them.

> *Greater love hath no man than this, that a man lay down his life for his friends.*
>
> (John 15:13)

All in all, friends, begin to see the good in people. My pastor often tells us to see Jesus in people. If we look hard enough for anything in a person we will find it. So instead of looking for a fault, sin or shortcoming why not look for the good? Always be willing to show mercy, forgiveness and encouragement in every situa-

49

tion whether we think the person deserves it or not. Seek the face of God, seek His presence, seek the filling of the Holy Ghost and seek His anointing to fall upon and rest upon you.

Take time out to search yourself. Do you find any resemblance to self-righteousness? If so, make a note of it. Will you openly confess it and repent from it?

_____

_____

_____

_____

CHAPTER FOUR

A Character of Faith

It is commonly known that believers of old were easily recognized because of their similar character of faith in a God that they trusted with every detail that encompassed their lives. Our spiritual ancestors were tough and could withstand the storms of life because of their faith in God. Their character was known to be one of always praying and looking to God, Whom they believed to be their source of strength, their Sustainer, Helper, and Provider. When all hell broke loose in their lives, they called on the only one who could help. They prayed, fasted, sang songs of the greatness and power of the God whom they believed was not dead but alive. Now character is a feature that helps us to identify, tell apart or be able to describe something or someone recognizably. And so we are able to differentiate those of us who have the character of the one who is called Faithful and those of us who do not because of our spiritual features. Our faith and faithfulness toward

Christ builds character in us – let's see how Romans 5:1-5 conveys this message:

Now that we have God's approval by faith, we have peace with God because of what our Lord Jesus Christ has done. Through Christ we can approach God and stand in his favor. So we brag because of our confidence that we will receive glory from God. But that's not all. We also brag when we are suffering. We know that suffering creates endurance, endurance creates character, and character creates confidence. We're not ashamed to have this confidence, because God's love has been poured into our hearts by the Holy Spirit, who has been given to us.

(Romans 5:1-5, GW)

Faith or faithfulness is one of the most important characteristics of a born again believer. This characteristic called faith becomes established when we believe on the Lord Jesus Christ. We must believe that Jesus Christ is the Son of God. We must believe that He was crucified, died and was buried as a propitiation for our sins. We must believe that on the third day He arose from the grave with all power in His hands. We must believe that He is now seated at the right hand of His Father, our Lord. We must believe that "He is" and that He is a rewarder of them that diligently seek Him. We must have at least that much faith. The Bible says that without this thing called faith it is impossible to please Him.

No one can please God without faith. Whoever goes to God must believe that God exists and that he rewards those who seek him.

(Hebrews 11:6, GW)

And so I am convinced that faith is the foremost and the first thing that we ought to have established. Once faith has been acquired it awakens the very soul of our being so that when we hear the Word and it is mixed with faith we can then obey the Lord and obeying is an act of faithfulness. It is absolutely awesome how God has designed this thing – Hebrews 4:2, KJV:

> *For unto us was the gospel preached, as well as unto them: but the word preached did not profit them, not being mixed with faith in them that heard it.*

> *We received the same promises as those people in the wilderness, but the promises didn't do them a bit of good because they didn't receive the promises with faith.*
>
> (Hebrews 4:2, MSG)

This means that faith must already be on the scene when the Word is heard in order for the believer's life to be fruitful – isn't that just awesome?

Faith will cause you to move all sorts of mountains in your life. With the faith we have we must believe His Word. Believe that the words of the Scriptures are true and that they were indeed inspired by the very God of peace Himself.

I began to search myself...I wondered if I had this characteristic of Christ whose life mine should pattern. Faith is the confident belief in the truth, value, or trustworthiness of a person, idea, or thing: assurance, belief, and certainty. Faith is belief that does not rest on logical proof or material evidence. Character is the combination of qualities or features that distinguishes one person, group, or thing from another. Moral quality constitutes the principles and motives that control the life and spirit.

When I put the two together I realized that I was coming up short. Christ's character spoke of the fruit of the Spirit, which is love, joy, peace, longsuffering, gentleness, goodness, faith, meekness, and temperance (Galatians 5:22-23 KJV). Remember that characteristic means a quality or feature that distinguishes one person, group or thing from another. The fruit of the Spirit is a feature that distinguishes a believer from a non-believer.

Let's talk about temperance/self-control, one of the components of the fruit of the Spirit. Dreadfully, so many of us who are believers lack this piece of the fruit. We are so out of control, so lawless in so many ways that we have failed to see. I experienced something so inspiring for this point: I was trying to read a notice on the Notice Board at my condominium. The paper had been torn and it was hanging upside down, so it was a little difficult to read. A resident came by and assisted me in turning the paper right side up so that I was able to read it, and even proceeded to read it for me. The notice stated that any cars that were parked in the fire lane for more than 10 minutes or parked on the grass or any other no parking area would be towed at the owner's expense. The helpful resident made a comment, quite to my amazement. He stated that it was foolish for them to put up such a notice (even though it was a requirement by the Police Department) and that I should not worry about obeying the rule. I was amazed at this incident because the mannerism of this person as I previously perceived it was one of calm and tranquility. I thought to myself, even the sweetest and most gentle-appearing one of us is so lawless – we are ever so ready to be uncontrollable, wild, and headstrong. We are so adamant about not being controlled by another person that we get out of control to make sure it doesn't happen.

Control of one's self or self-control is very essential to the believer. If we would just be able to keep our bodies under subjection, as Paul stated, it would keep us from falling into various works of the flesh - adultery, fornication, uncleanness, lustfulness, idolatry, sorcery, hatreds, fightings, jealousies, angers, rivalries, divisions, heresies, envyings, murders, drunkenness, and revelings. Many believers often have an excuse or is a reason for practicing the works of the flesh. It is always about what someone else has done wrong to them or not doing for them. But I beg to differ. According to the good book, the Bible, it is a lack of self-control that causes those who are confessing to be Christians, saved, born again, believers, etc. to practice the works of the flesh. Let's talk about a few of these for a minute.

Let's talk about several forms of sexual sins which are rampant in the church; adultery, masturbation (male and female), homosexuality and fornication; these acts are sinful and there is no justification for them. The fact that you may be single does not justify masturbation, sex, sexual games or innuendos with someone to whom you are not married. The fact that you are married and your spouse does not desire to be sexually active with you or is not able to be sexually active with you does not justify masturbation, or sex outside of your marriage. These sexual acts are the epitome of self-pleasure which is significantly contrary to biblical principles. If you find that you are involved in any of these sexual acts mentioned, or any works of the flesh you need to confess it and repent immediately – don't waste any time!!! God is longsuffering, but we ought not to frustrate His grace.

Another fruit of the Spirit of Christ that builds character is love. So many say that word so loosely yet without genuine devotion. I learned how to truly embrace people at my church. It is our custom, especially when we are parting at the end of a service, to embrace each other and say, "I love you," "God bless you," ect. The word *love* means a deep, tender, ineffable feeling of affection and solicitude toward a person, such as that arising from kinship, recognition of attractive qualities, or a sense of underlying oneness.

The Scripture tells us to have a **special love** for the household of faith – not a regular love, but a special love. Love demands action that says, "I will esteem your needs higher than mine."

Okay, someone wants to know, how does faith build character? Well, when you think of the word *build* it means to *increase or strengthen by adding gradually to something*. It also means to *develop or give form according to a plan or process*. When embarking upon any building project it is very important to consider what the task is going to require, and it is my belief (which is based on Scripture) that a person ought to do the same when considering the journey of being born again. Just as it is done in the natural so it should be done in the spirit.

Through Christ we can approach God and stand in his favor. So we brag because of our confidence that we will receive glory from God. But that's not all. We also brag when we are suffering. We know that suffering creates endurance, endurance creates character, and character creates confidence.

(Romans 5:2-4, GW)

And whoever does not bear his cross and come after me, he cannot be my disciple. For which of you, intending to build a tower, does not sit down first and count the cost, whether he may have enough to finish it; lest perhaps, after he has laid the foundation and is not able to finish, all those seeing begin to mock him, saying, This man began to build and was not able to finish. Or what king, going to make war against another king, does not first sit down and consult whether he is able with ten thousand to meet him who comes against him with twenty thousand? Or else, while the other is still a great way off, he sends a delegation and asks conditions of peace. So then, every one of you who does not forsake all his possessions, he cannot be my disciple.

(Luke 14:27-33, MKJV)

In order to tackle any building project you must have some tools to work with. Several of our very essential tools on this character – building project of the born again believer are *faith, obedience*, and *trust* in the Almighty. Okay, so we have our tools. We now need to count up the cost in order to build our character. The cost is as follows:

● Persecution – to pursue with hostile intent, to harass. *Remember what I told you: 'A servant isn't greater than his master.' If they persecuted me, they will also persecute you.*

(John 15:20, GW)

- Suffering – to tolerate or endure evil, injury, pain, to appear at a disadvantage. *For to you it is given on behalf of Christ not only to believe on Him, but also to suffer for His sake.*

  (Philipians 1:29)

- Tribulation – An experience that tests one's endurance, patience, or faith. *And not only so, but we glory in tribulations also: knowing that tribulation worketh patience; And patience, experience; and experience, hope.*

  (Romans 5: 3-4)

I recently read an article entitled, "Sanctified and Suffering," regarding women who were sanctified and suffering persecution and hostility at the hand of chauvinistic husbands and other male figures in the church. This article implied that this was just not the way of sanctification. The sanctified women's anthem, Proverbs 31, was dethroned. I replied to the editor, declaring that yes **sanctified is suffering** and provided Scripture references to verify my claims. I have experienced a whirlwind of insight since I replied to this article. I did mention in my reply that my sincere prayer goes out to these women who are suffering and that they would seek God's guidance in their situations because God did promise that He would provide us with a way of escape:

Be alert at all times. Pray so that you have the power to escape everything that is about to happen and to stand in front of the Son of Man.

(Luke 21:36, GW)

To be very honest with you, I don't like to suffer either, but the Scripture declares that we must suffer. Just as Jesus learned obedience through the things that He suffered, so will we; well, I know that I have. Had I not suffered some of the things that I have I would not have even an ounce of character today. I would be just as wishy-washy as I could be.

Please understand that by no means is it okay for a man, especially if he is confessing to be a born again believer, to raise his hand or fist at his wife. It is not condoned for a man to abuse his wife physically, emotionally, psychologically, spiritually, or mentally. Paul warns men to be very careful how they deal with women:

> *The same goes for you husbands: Be good husbands to your wives. Honor them, delight in them. As women they lack some of your advantages. But in the new life of God's grace, you're equals. Treat your wives, then, as equals so your prayers don't run aground.*
>
> (1 Peter 3:7, MSG)

If that doesn't do it here's another one for you.

> *...and whoever welcomes a child like this in my name welcomes me. These little ones believe in me. It would be best for the person who causes one of them to lose faith to be drowned in the sea with a large stone hung around his neck. How horrible it will be for the world because it causes people to lose their faith. Situations that cause people to lose their faith will arise. How horrible it will be for the person who causes someone to lose his faith!*
>
> (Matthew 18:5-7, GW)

Someone may be saying that there is no connection between the two Scriptures, but remember that He tells us that unless we become as a little child we **shall not enter** into the Kingdom of Hheaven – their were no exclusions. If I were like you and I were in the seat of the one who is being a bully or taking advantage of a woman's weakness, I would repent immediately, for it is a fearful thing to fall into the hands of the Living God (Hebrews 10:31).

Our faith in God causes us to be purpose-driven people, which is another character builder. Jesus had a purpose and His faith built that character in Him. He was not on this earth for Himself; He had come that sinners could have access to eternal life. That is why when He was tempted by the evil one He could activate His faith and apply the Word to every trick of the enemy. Had He been taken down He would not have fulfilled His purpose and His character would have been tainted. What about you today? We were created for a purpose; to be living witnesses of Christ in the earth and that character must be displayed in every area of our lives. Will you allow the character of Christ to eminate from you?

Remember Romans 8:18:

For I reckon that the sufferings of this present time are not worthy to be compared with the glory which shall be revealed in us.

2 Timothy 2:12:

If we suffer, we shall also reign with him: if we deny him, he also will deny us.

Okay let me break it down – Christ is the Head of the church and we the members will be treated with the same treatment as the Head. We are therefore united with Christ our Head in faith and as a result if we share in His sufferings, the persecutions, rejections, etc. then we also shall share in His triumphs. We will be glorified just as He is.

What about you friend, have you added to your faith? Is your salvation being built up in the faith of our Savior Jesus Christ, or are you in and out, up and down, sometimes enjoying being saved, sometimes not?

Add to your faith virtue; and to virtue knowledge; and to knowledge temperance; and to temperance patience; and to patience godliness; and to godliness brotherly kindness; and to brotherly kindness; charity. For if these things be in you, and abound, they make you that ye shall neither be barren nor unfruitful in the knowledge of our Lord Jesus Christ.

(2 Peter 1:5-8)

Can you identify areas and times in your life when you have refused to add to your faith? If yes, will you confess it and repent from it and commit to being a fruit-bearer instantly?

_____

_____

_____

_____

Chapter Five

Jesus Is the Only Remedy

For a born again believer, Jesus is the only remedy for the many challenges of life that we face. There is a very old and popular song that says, "Jesus is the answer for the world today, above Him there's no other, Jesus is the way!" For every situation that you can name or even begin to imagine, Jesus is the only remedy! There are so many descriptions for this one man, our Savior. He is known as a heart fixer, a mind regulator, a doctor, and a lawyer. Listen friend, He's the only one who can mend and bring healing to a broken relationship. When faced with tough decisions concerning marriage relationships, or any other relationship, the only recourse is Jesus...seeking His face. That is the only way that we will be made complete. That is the only way that we will be healed from the hurt and pain of the relationship. Friend, as born-again believers we ought to be able to be witnesses to our ex-spouses, spouses, pastors, family and friends.

How then can we say that we have the power of Christ living within us? But unfortunately we do say that we have this power but it is not being demonstrated in our lives. Jesus tells us to love our enemies, not to curse them but to love them.

Ye have heard that it hath been said, Thou shalt love thy neighbor, and hate thine enemy. But I say unto you, Love your enemies, bless them that curse you, do good to them that hate you, and pray for them which despitefully use you, and persecute you; That ye may be the children of your Father which is in heaven: for he maketh his sun to rise on the evil and on the good, and sendeth rain on the just and on the unjust. For if ye love them which love you, what reward have ye? Do not even the publicans the same? And if ye salute your brethren only, what do ye more than others? Do not even the publicans so? Be ye therefore perfect, even as your Father which is in heaven is perfect.

(Matthew 5:43-48)

What does love mean? It means to have a deep, tender, ineffable feeling of affection and solicitude toward a person: adoration, delight, and appreciation. And if our ex-spouses are behaving as our enemies or if our spouses are behaving as though they are the enemy, what then are we charged to do? LOVE them. Friends, we are charged to have a deep adoration and feeling of affection for those who are adversarial to us no matter who they are, and if we don't the Scripture says that we don't know God.

My beloved friends, let us continue to love each other, since love comes from God. Everyone who

*loves is born of God and experiences a relation-
ship with God. The person who refuses to love
doesn't know the first thing about God, because
God is love - so you can't know him if you don't
love.*

(1 John 4:7-8, MSG)

I understand, because I have been there myself.
You want to pet the hurt, you want to hurt just
because you are hurting, you want to find someone
who will empathize with you while you are hurting,
but after a while it is time to break camp. You have
been in mourning too long over that spouse, or that
relationship or that situation. The state that you are
in is not conducive to eternal or abundant life which
belongs to a born again believer. The state that you
are in is leading you to the path of death, because after
a while you will end up leaving your God. You may
not have left the church building, but it is quite possible to still be attending the church building but having abandoned your relationship with God.

There are those among us who'll say to a person
who has had a tragedy or loss in their life that they
need to get over it and there are those who'll say, "Its
easy for you to say get over it because you have not
had to go through what this person had to go
through." Which of these is true? The fact is that time
will heal the wound, but that doesn't mean that you
become incapacitated while you are waiting for the
wound to heal. Many people become spiritually com-
placent and even spiritually dead while waiting for
God to bring healing. They begin to use the hurt or
disappointment or loss or failure as a reason not to go
on. Listen, people of God, that is only a trick from our
enemy the devil. He does not want to see us live this

abundant life that Jehovah God has promised to us in the midst of all hell breaking loose. Guess what, God promised us that we would have abundant life if we abide in His Word and His Word abides in us; but He also promised that all who live godly shall suffer persecution.

Yea, and all that will live godly in Christ Jesus shall suffer persecution.

(2 Timothy 3:12)

There is no way around it. However, as Paul states, when we fall into these trials and tribulations we ought to count it all joy.

My brethren, count it all joy when ye fall into divers temptations; Knowing this, that the trying of your faith worketh patience.

(James 1:2-3)

There is a popular song by The Winans that relates to this Scripture and the words go like this – "Count it all joy even when it seems so hard to, no He'll never give you more than you can handle." In addition, we should also count it all joy knowing that God will not put more on us or will not allow us to fall into any situation that is too much for us to bear.

There hath no temptation taken you but such as is common to man: but God is faithful, who will not suffer you to be tempted above that ye are able; but will with the temptation also make a way to escape, that ye may be able to bear it.

(1 Corinthians 10:13)

How many years or how long after our spouse has left us, or we have experienced the death of a loved one, or some other form of loss or hurt should we wait to have joy in the Lord? According to the Scripture we are to have it right at that moment. I did not get the impression from Paul that there was a waiting period.

Someone may be saying in his or her mind that it is a cold and heartless thing to tell someone who has gone through a tragedy or loss that they have to get over it, but I am not the one who made up the rules. I am just like you; I have been commissioned to do His will to follow the rules. If you don't get over it, or strive to get over it, you'll become a stagnant Christian. As a matter of fact, you may even begin to draw back and that is not the appropriate remedy for the believer, because the Scriptures tell us that God has no pleasure in a person who withdraws;

Now, the just shall live by faith. But if he draws back, my soul shall have no pleasure in him.

(Hebrews 10:38, NKJV)

But we are not of those withdrawing to destruction, but of those who believe to the preserving of the soul.

(Hebrews 10:39, MKJV)

As tough as it may be, if we want to thrive or make it into the kingdom we must press forward.

Let's hear the Words of Jesus, our ultimate example and elder brother.

On the road someone asked if he could go along. "I'll go with you, wherever," he said. Jesus was curt: "Are you ready to rough it? We're not staying in the best inns, you know." Jesus said to another, "Follow me." He said,

67

"Certainly, but first excuse me for a couple of days, please. I have to make arrangements for my father's funeral." Jesus refused. "First things first. Your business is life, not death. And life is urgent: Announce God's kingdom!" Then another said, "I'm ready to follow you, Master, but first excuse me while I get things straightened out at home." Jesus said, "No procrastination. No backward looks. You can't put God's kingdom off till tomorrow. Seize the day."

(Luke 9:57-62, MSG)

Now why would Jesus say a thing like that? You see, if we are spending time nursing our wounds, frustrations, hurts, or disappointments, then we are not seizing the day, or redeeming the time.

Wherefore he saith, Awake thou that sleepest, and arise from the dead, and Christ shall give thee light. See then that ye walk circumspectly, not as fools, but as wise, redeeming the time, because the days are evil.

(Ephesians 5:14-16)

The bottom line is that we must remember that this world that we are living in is not our home. We are sojourners, we are traveling through, we are on our way to another city.

We don't have a permanent city here on earth, but we are looking for the city that we will have in the future.

(Hebrews 13:14, GW)

While we are here we must live as though this is not our home. We are just stewards over the things that God has entrusted into our hands. Our husbands are not ours; our wives, children, houses, possessions, land, etc. are not our own.

Have you made Jesus your only remedy for every aspect of your life including marital issues, children's issues, work issues, money issues, etc? Friend, if you are a born again believer you ought to look to Jesus and Him only and the statutes that He alone has implemented to remedy your everyday situations. He told us to lay our burdens upon Him. He is more than willing and able to take them and work them out for our good. Will you allow Him to remedy your situations today? Make a note of the steps that you plan to make and endeavour to follow them.

_____

_____

_____

_____

_____

_____

_____

_____

_____

CHAPTER SIX

Born Again to Overcome

Yea, though I walk through the valley of the shadow of death, I will fear no evil, for thou art with me.

(Psalm 23:4)

*A*s a born again believer we will walk through some valleys that seem to be meant for our death. These valleys seem as though they are going to take the very breath out of our bodies. But we are assured through the Word that God is with us; therefore we should not fear any evil. There shouldn't be any fear that the situation is for our demise but unfortunately that is usually our first response. However, here are some words from God through David that speak directly to us.

The LORD is my shepherd; I shall not want. He maketh me to lie down in green pastures: he leadeth me beside the still waters. He restoreth my soul: he leadeth me in the paths of right-eousness for his name's sake. Yea, though I walk through the valley of the shadow of death, I will fear no evil: for thou art with me; thy rod and thy staff they comfort me. Thou preparest a table before me in the presence of mine ene-mies: thou anointest my head with oil; my cup runneth over. Surely goodness and mercy shall follow me all the days of my life: and I will dwell in the house of the LORD forever.

(Psalm 23:1-6)

But now, GOD's Message, the God who made you in the first place, Jacob, the One who got you started, Israel: Don't be afraid, I've redeemed you. I've called your name. You're mine. When you're in over your head, I'll be there with you. When you're in rough waters, you will not go down. When you're between a rock and a hard place, it won't be a dead end.

(Isaiah 43:1-2, MSG)

I have had several attacks from the enemy since the inspiration of this book. The enemy does not want this information to get out because he knows that when truth comes, then the light of Christ becomes evident. It has taken me approximately four months to write this book and with every attack (and they have been numerous) something kept telling me, "There's no need to even write this book...what is writ-ten makes no sense and will not benefit anyone. What's the use? You should just stop writing, you should give up. What are you even writing about born again for? You're not born again." By the grace of God I have kept the faith, I will not be defeated, because God's only Son fought the battle and He won, and since the Holy Ghost came in and gave me power over sin, I will not be defeated anymore.

It is the utmost desire of Satan that all of God's creation is lost...but in the name of Jesus Christ of Nazareth, I declare war on the enemy. I will not be defeated; wounded though I am, I am going to fight till the end.

Whoever you are reading this book, I pray that you will take the same attitude. No matter what comes, hold on to the unchanging hand of Jesus the Christ. When the enemy fires his fiery darts, please hold up the shield of faith. These fiery darts are meant to kill the very Spirit of Christ within you – spiritual death – where Christ is no longer the center of your life. Satan's ultimate goal is "shoot to kill!" He does not intend to take any prisoners. If you don't believe that you have the shield of faith, ask the Almighty God to give it to you. Beseech Him, cry out to Him, call on Him, ask a prayer partner to help you call Him, run Him down...let Him know how urgent you are to receive it! He has promised that if you need more faith, all that you have to do is to ask and He will gladly give it. With this shield of faith you and I will be able to stand against the wiles (deceit, trickery, charm) of the devil. Satan is real!!! He truly wants to destroy our faith in the Christ who died so that our sins might be forgiven, and so that we might come to know and experience this abundant life. Listen, we are more than conquerors and we will always overcome because Christ has overcome this world and all of its devices, including the enemy of our soul, therefore we will also overcome.

These things I have spoken unto you, that in me ye might have peace. In the world ye shall have

tribulation: but be of good cheer; I have over-
come the world.

(John 16:33)

Because Christ has overcome the world and all of
its devices, we too are more than able to do the same.
We are more than conquerors and need not be defeated by our troubles and fears. Who shall separate us
from the love of Christ? Could oppression, or anguish,
or persecution, or famine, or nakedness, or peril, or
sword? Even as it is written, "For your sake we are
killed all day long. We were accounted as sheep for the
slaughter." No, in all these things, we are more than
conquerors through Him who loved us.

For I am persuaded, that neither death, nor
life, nor angels, nor principalities, nor things
present, nor things to come, nor powers, nor
height, nor depth, nor any other creature, shall
be able to separate us from the love of God,
which is in Christ Jesus our Lord.

(Romans 8:35-39)

Are you an overcomer, friend, or are you overcome
by the storms of your life, i.e., principalities, powers,
loss, hurt, disappointment and lack? We have a perfect example of One who has overcome the world – our
Savior Jesus Christ. What steps will you take to make
a change? What steps will you take in order to be an
overcomer?

_____

_____

_____

_____

CHAPTER SEVEN

Born Again to Praise

We show forth the glory of God when our walk is that of obeying His voice (not ours), hearing the Word and faithfully obeying by living holy and separated lives. Remember that holiness is not just what you wear or the places you no longer go to, etc., but it is your entire devotion to pleasing God. We were created to praise Him, to bless Him, to adore Him, and to glorify Him. We show forth His glory when we live lives that praise Him. He is glorified when we testify of His miracles, faithfulness, mercy, kindness and goodness.

My pastor recently preached a message entitled, "Why Should I Sing?" and the answer is "because He is good." We ought to testify and sing praises unto God wherever we are, just because He is good. We can then be like Habakkuk when he said,

Though the cherry trees don't blossom and the strawberries don't ripen, Though the apples are

worm-eaten and the wheat fields stunted, Though the sheep pens are sheepless and the cattle barns empty, I'm singing joyful praise to GOD. I'm turning cartwheels of joy to my Savior God. Counting on GOD's Rule to prevail, I take heart and gain strength. I run like a deer. I feel like I'm king of the mountain!
(Habakkuk 3:17-19, MSG)

David has left us with so many instructions on how to praise Him and why to praise Him and when to praise Him. Here are just a few, if you haven't already done so, you ought to make them a part of your daily homage unto Him:

Praise the LORD'S greatness with me. Let us highly honor his name together. I went to the LORD for help. He answered me and rescued me from all my fears.
(Psalm 34:3-4, GW)

Make a joyful noise to Jehovah, all you lands. Worship Jehovah with gladness; come before His presence with singing. Know that Jehovah, He is God. He has made us, and not we ourselves; we are His people, and the sheep of His pasture. Enter into His gates with thanksgiving, and into His courts with praise; be thankful to Him, and bless His name. For Jehovah is good; His mercy is everlasting; and His truth endures to all generations.
(Psalm 100:1-5, MKJV)

Hallelujah! Praise God in his holy place. Praise him in his mighty heavens. Praise him for his mighty acts. Praise him for his immense greatness. Praise him with sounds from horns.

Praise him with harps and lyres. Praise him with tambourines and dancing. Praise him with stringed instruments and flutes. Praise him with loud cymbals. Praise him with crashing cymbals.   Let everything that breathes praise the LORD! Hallelujah!

(Psalm 150:1-6, GW)

You see, if we do anything other than that we diminish the awesomeness of God in our lives – we praise Him when the bills are paid and relationships and other situations seem to be going just right, but refuse to open our lips and lift our voices in glad adoration when it seems like our world is falling to pieces. Friends, we were created to praise His name and that is where He dwells. He does not dwell in depression, resentment, disappointment, unforgiveness, stubbornness, disobedience, slothfulness, or faithlessness. He dwells in the midst of our praise and as a born-again believer the very God whom we say that we are serving ought to be dwelling in the midst of us, therefore **we ought to praise Him**! What about you, will you commit to praising God and being worshipful before Him?

_____

_____

_____

_____

_____

CHAPTER EIGHT

It's Time to Clean House

Don't you realize that your body is a sacred place, a place where the Holy Spirit dwells? Don't you see that you can't live however you please, squandering what God paid such a high price for? The price was the death of His Son Jesus. God owns the whole works. So let people see God in and through your body.

(1 Corinthians 6:19-20 paraphrased)

At least once per week, most people clean their physical house because over the course of the week dust builds up, the mirrors get foggy or stained with splashes of water, rings begin to form around the toilet, the floors become soiled, the carpet retains the dirt from the shoes and any other particles that may have fallen on it, and so on. If the house is not clean when guests come over they will be disgusted, at least to see the condition of the home and will not want to stay very long because your home is not one that is visitor friendly. And so it is with the house where the Spirit of Christ resides. As the Scripture says we cannot live just any way that pleases us or that is comfortable, we should live so that we are visitor friendly. We ought to be visitor friendly to our brothers and sisters in Christ and to those who are lost. And so we must **clean house** every now and again to make sure that we are visitor friendly.

It doesn't matter how long you have been confessing salvation, if you find that you have been walking in some of the works of the flesh that have been mentioned, then it behooves you to begin to clean house. The ultimate goal is that when we die or when we get to the judgment seat, we want to hear the Almighty say, "Well done thou good and faithful servant, enter ye into my rest."

How do we clean house? We must constantly take note of our attitudes. We can't allow an attitude or spirit of unforgiveness, for example, to stay with us. To be honest with you, letting it stay one minute is long enough. When we allow these spirits to stay with us too long they become too comfortable and when they become comfortable they begin to invite other like spirits to join them. Once a spirit of unforgiveness comes in we must be willing to strive with all that God Himself has empowered us with to get rid of this guest. We must fast and pray. We must acknowledge it. We must confess it. We must repent and make a conscious effort to keep our house clean from this spirit.

I declare that as long as we are in these earthly bodies we will need to continue to clean house. We cannot for a moment presume that we are in such a right standing with God, otherwise we will be in a state that we are stinking and not even be aware of it. We must do as Paul states in Philippians 3:12, MSG:

> *I'm not saying that I have this all together, that I have it made. But I am well on my way, reaching out for Christ, Who has so wondrously reached out for me.*

Friends, don't get me wrong: By no means do I count myself an expert in all of this, but I've got my eye on the goal, where God is beckoning us onward to Jesus.

It amazes me how we – saints of the Most High God, take so long to get rid of the ills in our lives. The Scripture says that these kinds only come out by fasting and praying, so we know what the remedy is for getting rid of the attitudes in our lives that do not produce good fruit. Why do we wait so long to get rid of them? We allow them to linger around for so long until spiritual death begins to manifest itself in our lives.

Friend, it is imperative for us to come clean. We need to begin to confess our sins as the Scripture says. We have sugar-coated so many things in our lives that are hindering us from having a right relationship with God. It is time to begin to recognize those things that are hindering us from serving God with fervor and joy.

In many Holy Ghost-filled and anointed churches we have a time after the Word is preached for those who would like to receive salvation or for those who want prayer to come and receive it. I challenge you to be courageous, and instead of asking for prayer for a new car, job, house, husband, etc. that you ask for prayer for deliverance, ask for a change of heart and do it from your heart. So many of you are suffering from so much hostility, anger, depression, resentment, guilt, unforgiveness; you name it, you've got it, and you've buried it. Saints, things that are buried stink after a while. We then become whitewashed sepulchers full of dead men's bones, as Jesus puts it. The outside will be all dressed up in finely tailored suits and dresses and hats and shoes and purses to match, and makeup well put together but inside we are hating people and God, we are angry at people and God.

I challenge you to bring those buried hurts to the surface so that you can be delivered from them once and for all and you can serve God the way you ought to with joy and gladness. Don't worry about what people are going to think about you, your salvation and relationship with God depends on your coming clean and it is more valuable than what some nay-sayer might think about you. I promise you that once you begin to allow God to clean you up you'll experience such a joy in serving the Lord that you've never experienced before – I know because He's done it for me and keeps right on doing it.

On the first Saturday of every month the ladies in my church gather at one of our sister's homes. We were inspired by the Holy Spirit through Acts 2, where the believers gathered from house to house sharing their meals together with singleness of heart. I remember being delivered from a melancholy spirit, being unmerciful, anger, just to name a few. And I know of other testimonies of healing and deliverance and salvation. But the key point is that these ills had to be voiced; they had to be revealed. I could have hidden it but I recognized that I had a problem. I would drift off into a melancholy state at times and I confessed it to my sisters and declared that I did not want to go back there anymore, and I haven't since, by the grace of God. What is yours? What is the chain that holds you captive? Is it fear? Is it anger? Is it witchcraft? Confess it, and declare to yourself that you are not going back into that area anymore.

There is a song that says, "Search me, O God, and know my heart today, try me, O Savior, know my thoughts I pray. See if there be some wicked way in me. Cleanse me from every sin and set me free." This must be our prayer to the Lord on a regular basis, because sometimes there are some things that we have buried deep within and only a purging from the Lord can reveal it and set you free from it. It is time to consecrate a fast and seek the Lord to clean house.

Be honest with God, because nothing is hidden from Him anyway. When you begin to pray come before the Lord humbly, acknowledge that He is God and that He is faithful to His Word. Seek His mercy and His undeserving grace. Without being ostentatious express your fears, desires, deepest darkest most shameful tendencies. Confess your sins unto Him. It's time to take a deep look inside yourself and see if there be any traces of self-righteousness or ingratitude or any other unrighteous act in your life. Be very serious about this, because this is the only way that you will be able to embrace the freedom that Christ has sacrificed His life for. Once you've identified those areas, then I want you to make a conscious effort to do something about it.

CONFESS IT AND FORGET IT

Make this your common practice: Confess your sins to each other and pray for each other so that you can live together whole and healed. The prayer of a person living right with God is something powerful to be reckoned with.

(James 5:16, MSG)

Confess it and forget it simply means that once you've confessed it and repented of the sin, God declares that He remembers our sins no more, so if God does not remember them, then why should you? Your neighbor might remember it but in order for you to progress in your walk with Christ you must do as Paul says,

But this one thing I do, forgetting those things which are behind, and reaching forth unto those things which are before, I press toward the mark for the prize of the high calling of God in Christ Jesus.

(Philippians 3:13-14)

What area(s) have you identified? Are you holding any animosity toward a parent that you feel neglected you as a child? Are you angry with a spouse for being unfaithful (committing adultery/divorce)? Are you resentful toward a spouse because you feel that you are at a disadvantage? Are you holding a grudge against a friend or someone who was once a friend? What about the loss of a loved one, is that weighing you down? Have you found it difficult to forgive? Are you envious of someone's relationship or position or talent or influence? I may not have identified yours but once you have identified it, write it down. Make a list of all that is revealed to you, whether it is a recent or a past incident.

_____

_____

_____

_____

_____

Now that you have identified the dirt and the clutter, what steps will you take to clean house - be delivered from it? Make a commitment to yourself and to God to faithfully use every holy and righteous means possible to walk in liberty not just for this moment but continually!

_____

_____

_____

_____

_____

If you've done just that, I say unto you in the words of Jesus,

Go thy way and sin no more and LIVE ABUNDANTLY!!!